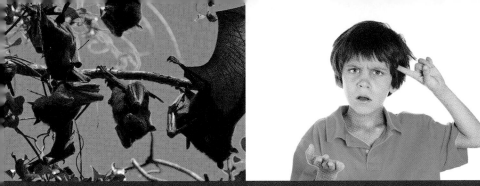

Tell Me Why

WHY?

Bats Sleep Upside Down

Susan H. Gray

Published in the United States of America by Cherry Lake Publishing
Ann Arbor, Michigan
www.cherrylakepublishing.com

Content Adviser: Bruce W. Miller PhD and Carolyn M. Miller MSc., conservation biologists who studied bats at Chan Chich Lodge (Gallon Jug Estate, Belize), funded by the Wildlife Conservation Society
Reading Adviser: Marla Conn, ReadAbility Inc

Photo Credits: © Sebastian Burel/Shutterstock Images, cover, 1, 15; © Kushal Bose/Shutterstock Images, cover, 1, 21; © Adi Ciurea/Shutterstock Images, 11; © StevenRussellSmithPhotos/Shutterstock Images, 5; © Nature Diver/Shutterstock Images, 7; © Kirsanov Valeriy Vladimirovich/Shutterstock Images, 9; © Maksimilian/Shutterstock Images, cover, 1, 13; © Gucio_55/Shutterstock Images, 17; © Maxim Tarasyugin/Shutterstock Images, 19

Library of Congress Cataloging-in-Publication Data

Gray, Susan Heinrichs, author.
  Bats sleep upside down / Susan H. Gray.
    pages cm.—(Tell me why)
  Summary: "Young children are naturally curious about animals. Bats Sleep Upside Down offers answers to their most compelling questions about why bats hang upside-down at night. Age-appropriate explanations and appealing photos encourage readers to continue their quest for knowledge. Additional text features and search tools, including a glossary and an index, help students locate information and learn new words"—Provided by publisher.
  Audience: Ages 6–10
  Audience: K to grade 3.
  Includes bibliographical references and index.
  ISBN 978-1-63362-608-9 (hardcover)—ISBN 978-1-63362-698-0 (pbk.)—ISBN 978-1-63362-788-8 (pdf)—ISBN 978-1-63362-878-6 (ebook) 1. Bats—Juvenile literature. 2. Bats—Behavior—Juvenile literature. 3. Children's questions and answers. I. Title. II. Series: Tell me why (Cherry Lake Publishing)

QL737.C5G685 2015
599.4—dc23

2014047991

Cherry Lake Publishing would like to acknowledge the work of the Partnership for 21st Century Skills. Please visit *www.p21.org* for more information.

Printed in the United States of America
Corporate Graphics

Table of Contents

The Bat House

Ryan was helping his dad in the workshop. His father was always building things. Last month, Ryan had helped him build two birdhouses. Together, they nailed them to trees in the backyard. Now, Ryan's dad had some new plans. They were going to make a bat house. It would be a safe place for bats to sleep.

Bats are common animals in the United States, but people rarely see them because they are most active at night.

All afternoon, they sawed, nailed, and glued. Ryan could see the house coming together. It looked a lot like a big birdhouse. He imagined bats sleeping safely inside.

Finally, his father held up the house and said, "It's done!" Ryan's jaw dropped. His dad must have lost his mind. The house had four nice, smooth sides and a roof. But inside, the walls and ceiling were very rough. And the floor was completely missing! What was his dad thinking?

Look at this bat house. How is it different from a birdhouse? How do bats get in and out of it?

Building a bat house will attract bats to your yard.

A Bat's Life

Ryan's dad saw the confused look on his son's face. "Come into the house," he said. "I have a new book about bats. Let's read it together. I think you'll see why our bat house looks this way."

His father opened the book and began to read. "Bats are **mammals**. They are covered with short hair. The skin on their wings is very thin. Bats have tiny feet, and their toes have claws."

Considering its small body size, this bat has a very wide wingspan.

Ryan's dad went on. "Bats are **nocturnal**, so they sleep during the day and are active at night. Most of them fly around catching insects. Some eat fruit or **nectar**. And some eat small birds and mice. As the night ends, they head home. Some sleep in caves or under bridges. Others sleep in trees or bat houses. They swoop in and grab a spot with their feet. They cling to their **foothold** and let their bodies dangle. Then they fall asleep."

Ask your school librarian to help you find books on bats. See if you can learn more about their lives.

This greater horseshoe bat is sleeping in a cave.

Hanging Around

Like birds, bats are flying animals. But bats do not fly the same way birds do. Their takeoffs are completely different. Birds leap or get a "running start" before rising into the air. Bats are built a different way. They usually crawl instead of walk. Their knees bend backward. Their movements are clumsy. So, from the ground, they just cannot lift themselves into the air.

Bats' bodies are not built for walking.

The bat solves this problem by hanging high off the ground. When it is ready to fly, the bat simply lets go. As it drops, it begins to flap its wings. It quickly rotates its body so it is upright. The bat does not need a running start. It does not have to rise into the air. It is already up in the air from the start.

This fruit bat is about to start flying.

A bat may sleep upside down for hours. You'd think its feet would get tired and let go. But bats have special toes. Once a bat gets a foothold, its body swings down and dangles. The weight of the body pulls on **tendons** that run to the toes. The tendons pull the toes into a curl that grips the foothold until the bat wants to let go.

What if a bat found itself on the ground? How could it get up to a high place without flying?

This fruit bat's super-strong toes let it hang upside down for a long time.

17

Some Other Hangers

Bats are not the only animals that sleep upside down. **Sloths** are mammals that spend most of their time hanging from tree limbs. They eat, sleep, and carry their babies while dangling upside down. **Opossums** also hang with their heads down. They do not hang by their feet, though. They cling to tree limbs with their tails. Opossums can hang this way for only a short time. They may climb trees to escape predators, but they do not sleep in this position.

Sloths also spend a lot of time hanging upside down.

State parks are great places to learn more about bats. Those that offer cave tours are especially good. Tour leaders can answer your questions about bats. They can tell you which bat **species** live there. They know what time bats come out at night. They can explain how to build a bat house. And they will certainly know why bats sleep upside down!

The Congress Avenue Bridge has more than a million bats living underneath it and coming out each summer night.

Think About It!

Bats sleep during the day. But some daytime animals such as hawks eat them. How do bats stay safe from such dangers?

People build bat boxes and plant gardens that attract bats. Why would someone want bats living nearby?

Insect-eating bats must catch their food in flight. How can they do this in the dark? Ask a teacher to help you find the answer.

Glossary

foothold (FOOT-hold) a safe place where feet can be planted

mammals (MAM-uhlz) animals that have hair or fur and usually give birth to live babies

nectar (NEK-tur) a sweet liquid from a plant

nocturnal (nahk-TUR-nuhl) active at night

opossums (uh-POSS-umz) small mammals with a pouch for carrying their young

sloths (SLAWTHS) very slow-moving mammals that live in trees

species (SPEE-seez) one type, or kind, of plant or animal

tendons (TEN-duhnz) dense bands of tissue that connect muscles to bones

Find Out More

Books:

Carney, Elizabeth. *Bats*. Washington, DC: National Geographic Society, 2010.

Johnson, J. Angelique. *Bats*. North Mankato, MN: Capstone Press, 2011.

Mattern, Joanne. *It's a Good Thing There Are Bats*. Danbury, CT: Children's Press, 2014.

Web Sites:

Bats4Kids: Bats Bats Everywhere
www.bats4kids.org
Read more about bats' lives and behavior.

Organization for Bat Conservation: Kid's Page
www.batconservation.org/education/educational-resources/kids-page
Look here to find instructions for attracting bats and for building a bat house.

Animal Tourism: Where to See Bats
www.animaltourism.com/animals/bat.php
Look at this map to see if you can observe bats in the wild near where you live, or somewhere you are visiting.

Index

About the Author

Susan H. Gray has a master's degree in zoology. She has worked in research and has taught college-level science classes. Susan has also written more than 140 science and reference books, but especially likes to write about animals. She and her husband, Michael, live in Cabot, Arkansas.